CARRILLO

AMERICAN HISTORY TOPIC BOOKS

THE FOUNDING OF THE REPUBLIC

Richard B. Morris

Illustrations by Leonard Everett Fisher

Lerner Publications Company   Minneapolis

For Deborah,
whose felicitous choice of parents guarantees her
firm grounding in the traditions and values of
the American Republic

1985 REVISED EDITION

Revised edition copyright © 1985 by Lerner Publications Company.
Published by arrangement with Lou Reda Productions, Inc.
First published as *The First Book of the Founding of the Republic.*

Library of Congress Cataloging in Publication Data

Morris, Richard Brandon, 1904-
      The founding of the Republic.

     (American history topic books)
     Rev. ed. of: The first book of the founding of the
Republic 1968.
     Includes index.
     Summary: Surveys the decisive years, 1789-1801, of
the American Republic when the leadership of the
Federalists formed a solid base for the government and
the future of a nation.
     1. United States — History — Constitutional period,
1789-1809 — Juvenile literature. [1. United States —
History — Constitutional period, 1789-1809]
I. Fisher, Leonard Everett, ill.   II. Morris, Richard
Brandon, 1904-   . First book of the founding of
the Republic. III. Title. IV. Series.
E310.M87 1985   973.4'1   85-12934
ISBN 0-8225-1704-3 (lib. bdg.)

Manufactured in the United States of America

     2 3 4 5 6 7 8 9 10 94 93 92 91 90 89 88 87 86

Contents

Introduction to Revised Edition

☆☆ The framers of the Constitution had written a remarkable document, and the people had approved it. Still a big question remained. Could the republic that had been created on paper preserve order and win the loyalty of millions of Americans who inhabited a territory larger than that of any republic since the days of Rome?

This question was soon answered. The new republic would prosper because of its superb leaders. The nation's first president, George Washington, commanded the affection and respect of the whole country. He chose some of the nation's best minds to run the departments of the government. Washington picked the talented Alexander Hamilton to be secretary of the treasury and the learned and experienced Thomas Jefferson as secretary of state. He named John Jay to be the first chief justice. In Congress, Washington leaned heavily on the advice of James Madison, who quickly pushed through the Bill of Rights and quieted the fears of the people that the new government might threaten their liberties.

In just a dozen years, the Federalists, as Washington's followers were called, had made the Constitution a workable instrument of government. During those years the two presidents — Washington and his successor, John Adams — shaped the powers and set the traditions of the presidential office. A cabinet system, not mentioned in the Constitution, came into being. The government used its ability to levy and collect taxes and to borrow money to put the nation's credit on a firm foundation.

Washington's decision to stay out of the European war that spread during the French Revolution kept the country stable and prosperous. Hamilton, who favored staying out, and Jefferson, who was more sympathetic to France, divided over this issue as well as over questions of domestic policy. Out of that conflict arose an opposition party. When the Constitution was drafted, political parties were considered a source of trouble. Today we welcome the existence of opposing parties as a true test of democracy.

Although the Federalist Era officially ended when Jefferson and his opposition party swept into office in 1800, many of the policies of the Federalists were continued. Truly the early founders had laid a solid foundation for the future of the republic.

The Federalists Take the Stage

☆☆ IT WAS 1789 — A YEAR OF NEW BEGINNINGS FOR THE YOUNG United States of America. After two years of hard thinking and debate among the citizens, a new Constitution had been agreed upon. Would it work?

If there were doubters, it might be said that history partly supported their viewpoint. One form of government — a loose binding together of the states under a constitution called the Articles of Confederation — had proved too weak to deal with the many problems of the new nation. It had failed. Now the testing time had come for the new Constitution and for the new President whose election it provided for.

Those who had hopes for the new government could point

1

to one enormous asset. In 1789, a remarkable group of men came into power in America. They did not use their power to enslave others or to make great fortunes for themselves. They devoted themselves wholeheartedly to building a nation that would win the respect of its citizens and of the rest of the world.

The group of people who governed the nation in the years from 1789 to 1801 were called the Federalists. They had fought hard for the adoption of the federal Constitution and were now determined to see that it should succeed. They were strong-minded men, very unlike one another as human beings and not afraid to express their differences. Some of them did not remain Federalists but in time formed an opposition party. Still, despite their differences, the Federalists together made a great record.

Washington Is Elected

☆☆ EVERYBODY TOOK IT FOR GRANTED THAT GEORGE WASHINGton would be the first President of the nation. Still, he had to be elected to that office. As is true today, the President was chosen by electors from each state. In some states, the people voted for presidential electors. In other states, the legislatures chose them. And in at least one state, the governor and his council picked the electors. The Constitution provided that each elector was to vote for two people. The person who received the highest number of all the votes cast—if it made a majority— would be President; the one who received the next highest would be Vice President. In case of a tie, the election would be thrown into the House of Representatives, where each state would have one vote in the final election of the President.

There really was no contest about who would be President but, curiously enough, there was some doubt as to who would be Vice President. Alexander Hamilton wanted to be sure that there would be no hitch and that George Washington would get more votes than the second candidate, John Adams. Hamilton saw to it that in some states votes were cast for others than Adams — for John Jay or George Clinton, both of New York, for instance. Hamilton had little reason to worry. When the electors cast their ballots, Washington was unanimously chosen. Adams ran far behind, and there was a sprinkling of votes for a few other candidates.

George Washington left the peace and quiet of his beloved home, Mount Vernon, with real regret. He started on a triumphal tour to the nation's capital, which was then New York. As the tour began, he remarked that he felt like "a culprit who is going to the place of his execution." He realized how difficult his task would be and how little thanks he would receive from people of ill will, but he accepted the call as a duty that he owed to his country.

Yet, for the moment, his heart was gladdened by the cheers of the crowds all along the route from Mount Vernon to New York. He was given so many salutes, parades, and banquets that it took him a week to reach New York. At Trenton, flowers were strewn in his path. A barge was built to carry him from New Jersey to New York Harbor. As he approached the Battery in New York, he was greeted by a thirteen-gun salute, and another salute was sounded from the foot of Wall

Street, where Washington left the barge and disembarked onto a pair of carpeted steps. That night, the town was ablaze with bonfires, and the skies were lighted up with fireworks.

On April 30, 1789, after attending church, the President-elect was escorted to Federal Hall at the junction of Broad and Wall streets for his inauguration. Chancellor Robert R. Livingston of New York recited the oath. Washington repeated: "I do solemnly swear that I will faithfully execute the office of President of the United States and will, to the best of my ability, preserve, protect, and defend the Constitution of the United States." Washington added, "So help me, God." He then bent and kissed the Bible. After he had taken the oath, the new President stepped out onto the balcony overlooking Wall Street. Dressed in a dark brown suit, white silk stockings, shoes with silver buckles, and with a huge steel-hilted sword at his side, he was a heroic-looking figure. The people shouted, "Long live George Washington!" Church bells pealed. The first President of the new nation had taken office.

George
Washington

Washington – a Man of Judgment and Character

☆☆ SOMEONE HAS CALLED GEORGE WASHINGTON A "MONU-ment rather than a man," and the Washington Monument in our national capital is evidence of his hold on the American people. But the America of his day knew him also as a great man. He quickly won not only respect for himself and his office but also loyalty to the United States Constitution, whose adoption many people had bitterly opposed. The country knew George Washington as a man who could manage other men, who could make long-range plans, and who was careful down to the tiniest detail.

Washington believed that the national government had to be strengthened and that the union of the states had to be made firm. The President realized that, to achieve this great goal, the nation had to build up its economic life and remain at peace. Washington was not a trained diplomat. He was not an expert in money matters. But he knew how to pick able men and how to take advice from them without giving up any of his authority.

When Washington took office, one of the first questions that arose was how to address the President. He was the head of state, and he was to be dealt with courteously. At the same time, the new nation was a republic and did not want to create the impression that a king had been set up on a throne. The Senate considered the matter. One senator suggested that the President be called "his Highness." Another suggested humorously that the Vice President be called "his Rotundity." He was referring to the fact that John Adams was short and stocky. The question was settled by the House of Representatives, which decided to address the President as "George Washington, President of the United States." That title has come down to us in shortened form as "Mr. President."

Washington looked the part of a President. He was commanding, but aloof and formal. He ran afternoon receptions called levees. These were rather stiff affairs. The President, dressed in black velvet, and wearing gloves and carrying a cocked hat, bowed to visitors, but shook hands with no one. On the other hand, on Fridays, George's wife, Martha, ran very pleasant social evenings that were less formal occasions.

Washington was able to remain dignified without losing touch with the people. During his first two years in office, he

8

The President bowed to visitors.

toured New England and the South and was able to find out
for himself the state of the union as well as the problems of the
American people who made it up.

Building the Machinery of Government

☆☆ DURING THE SUMMER AND EARLY FALL OF 1789, CONGRESS set up three departments. They were Foreign Affairs, Treasury, and War. In addition, the office of Postmaster General was held over from earlier times, and the office of Attorney General was established. Shortly thereafter, the Department of Foreign Affairs was renamed the State Department.

In the same session, Congress set up the Supreme Court. It had a Chief Justice of the United States and five Associate Justices. Washington named John Jay as the first Chief Justice. Jay was the New York lawyer who had served in the Confederation as Secretary for Foreign Affairs. Jay's court upheld the powers of the national government under the Constitution.

John
Jay

12

Congress also established thirteen federal district courts and three circuit courts. The Constitution, in Article III, states what the powers and duties of these federal courts shall be.

The framers of the Constitution laid down some general principles of government but did not intend to draw a detailed blueprint that would cover all the operations of the government for all future ages. As a result of practices that soon developed, a body of unwritten customs arose. We sometimes call these customs the "unwritten constitution." Here are a few examples of it.

The Constitution says that the President has the power to make treaties and appointments "by and with the advice and consent of the Senate." Washington went to the Senate to get their advice, but that body would not receive him. As a result, he no longer sought their advice but, once a treaty had been drawn up or an official appointed, merely asked their approval, or consent. Later Presidents have followed the same procedure. They make the treaties and certain appointments; the Senate ratifies them.

Early in Washington's administration, Congress called on the President to let them look at certain confidential papers. George Washington refused to turn the papers over to Congress. In so doing, he upheld the doctrine of "separation of powers." By this doctrine, the executive, the legislative, and the judicial branches of the government each operate in separate and distinct spheres, and the powers of one branch over another are greatly limited.

The most important example of the unwritten constitution

is the existence of the Cabinet. The Cabinet is not mentioned in the Constitution, which merely speaks of heads of departments. Very soon after he took office, Washington began to consult each of the heads of departments personally. Later he gathered these men together as a group every now and then, and talked over his policies. The group is known as the Cabinet. Ever since Washington's time, Cabinet officers have met with the President more or less regularly.

Hamilton Against Jefferson

☆☆ WASHINGTON'S CABINET HAD SOME STRONG PERSONALITIES. There was elephantine Henry Knox, the Secretary of War, who had also served in that capacity under the Articles of Confederation. There was Edmund Randolph, the rather eccentric Attorney General, who had come to the support of the Constitution rather late in the day. For Postmaster General, Washington appointed Samuel Osgood, but this post was not considered a Cabinet position at that time.

Two great figures loomed largest of all in Washington's Cabinet. They were Alexander Hamilton, who became Secretary of the Treasury, and Thomas Jefferson, who became Secretary of State. Only a man as great as Washington would have dared to put in one Cabinet two men whose views and personalities were seemingly so contrasting.

Alexander Hamilton had come to America from the West Indies on the eve of the Revolution. He had been born in poverty and throughout his life he seemed to search out ways to bury some of the less pleasant memories of his childhood. He stood at the center of events for almost twenty years and had a special talent for making enemies. He was accused of being a monarchist — that is, of favoring a king for America. He was denounced as a crook. He was attacked as a man who opposed the people.

But his admirers — and there were many of them — saw him in very different clothes. George Washington considered him an extremely bright and gifted young man — ambitious, but only in desiring to excel in whatever he set out to do.

The most important idea that Hamilton contributed to the new republic was his belief in the destiny of America. "Think continentally," he counseled the young nation. These words were a reminder to the people to think of themselves as rulers of a great territory, not a narrow strip of land along the Atlantic coast. Hamilton wished to confer upon the national government enough power so that it could fulfill its great mission.

Alexander Hamilton had an inventive mind and a bold one. He dealt with an amazing range of problems. As Secretary of the Treasury, he was anxious to see that faith in America's ability to pay its debts was firmly established at home and abroad. He was not the kind of person to sit back while business was suffering or was being harmed by importations of cheap foreign goods. He believed strongly in private business, but he also believed that private business could flourish only if the government had a direct hand in economic life. For that reason, he favored tariffs on imported goods and also favored the government's building canals, roads, and other public works.

Above all, Hamilton was a genius at administration — perhaps the greatest such genius that America has yet produced. He believed in having a strong President, and, with this belief, he devoted himself in the Cabinet to making sure that the President's powers would be ample. He concerned himself with every phase of public policy, acting more like a prime minister than a Secretary of the Treasury.

In some respects, Hamilton was a great success, but in others, he was a failure. He opened himself to criticism by boldly leading the attack on his foes. He did not understand how to compromise. He did not understand party politics. There is a time to talk and a time to be quiet. Hamilton knew when to talk but not when to be quiet. He was too open and too critical, even of his colleagues. Truly, Hamilton, a great man with a great talent, was a difficult colleague to have in the Cabinet.

Thomas Jefferson had started out in life with all the things that Hamilton lacked in childhood. Jefferson came from a family of gentry. He was accustomed to gracious living; he was rooted in the soil of his native Virginia. While Hamilton was short, Jefferson was lanky. The Secretary of the Treasury was a somewhat dandified dresser; the Virginian was sometimes very sloppy about the way he looked. When Jefferson was President later on, one senator who called on him at the White House mistook him for the butler.

Thomas Jefferson may have looked like a country squire, but he had an astonishing variety of talents. He was a learned lawyer. He could play the violin. He invented all sorts of gadgets. He was famous as an architect, and he took scientific farming very seriously.

Hamilton and Jefferson have come to stand for two opposite points of view in American life. Hamilton stood for central power in government and for business enterprise, and he had very little faith in the wisdom of ordinary people. Jefferson believed that there should be limits to the power of the federal government. He was less interested in the businessman and favored the farmer. He was deeply concerned about civil rights and was very anxious that the new republic should become a democracy, where the people would govern. It has been said that Jefferson was shrewd enough to back the causes for which time was fighting.

In fact, too much has been made of the differences between these two great leaders. When, as President, Jefferson acquired the vast Louisiana Territory from France, he acted as Hamilton probably would have. "Every difference of opinion is not a difference of principle," Jefferson would remind us. Alexander Hamilton wanted a government that could act. And — as a later President, Woodrow Wilson, pointed out — we can no longer accept Jefferson's idea that the best government is the government that does as little governing as possible. Wars, injustice, and poverty have forced modern governments to do a

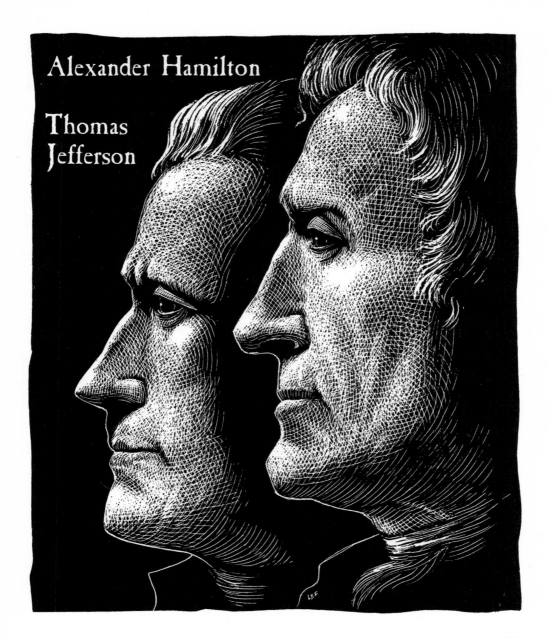

Alexander Hamilton

Thomas Jefferson

19

great deal to remedy poor conditions — certainly to do vastly more than in 1790. When people look to their government for help, they are paying tribute to Alexander Hamilton. Today both the great American political parties have accepted Hamilton's view that the central government must have the power to act. And too, both political parties accept Jefferson's views that the goal of government is a free society.

Both Hamilton and Jefferson left their stamp on the kind of nation that America has become.

Hamilton Has a Program:
Paying Off Debts

☆☆ HAMILTON STUDIED BUSINESS CONDITIONS IN THE NEW RE-public and found that both the United States and the original thirteen states were heavily in debt. These large debts had swollen in the course of fighting the American Revolution and winning independence from the English. Hamilton realized that people could not borrow money if they were known not to pay their bills. The people who had money to lend would not trust them. Another word for "trust" is "credit." For Hamilton, a nation's credit was just as important as an individual's. Unless a nation had credit, it could not become prosperous, and it could not be considered honorable in its dealings with other nations.

21

When Hamilton looked around him, he saw a nation living under a blanket of debt. The debt of the federal government amounted to over fifty million dollars. The states owed perhaps half as much. In all, for those days, this was an enormous debt to be borne by a nation of only four million persons.

In his first report to Congress, Hamilton proposed that all the debts inherited from the Confederation be paid in full by the central government. His proposal created something of a stir. Nobody objected to paying off the foreign debt — the money that had been borrowed from other countries. The domestic debt, however, was a different story. In order to get money to pay for fighting the Revolution, the states had borrowed from private citizens and in return had given them bonds, promising to repay the money with interest within a certain time. In the difficult days after the war, many of the veterans of the American Revolution, short of money, had been obliged to sell these bonds to speculators at ridiculously low prices. As a result, many of the bondholders in 1790 had only recently purchased their state certificates, but they were the ones who would now gain a profit from them.

No one was more outraged at the proposal that the federal government should pay the domestic debts than James Madison of Virginia. He had fought at Hamilton's side to secure the adoption of the Constitution. He had joined Hamilton and John Jay in writing the famous *Federalist* essays, arguing for a stronger Union. Now he and Hamilton were at odds over the question of the debt. Madison championed the "hardy veterans" who had been forced to sell their claims against the government for a song. He would have given the original bond-holders a share of the profits gained by the new bondholders. In practice, this might have been a little complicated to carry out. Congress thought so, and adopted Hamilton's plan.

Another question was whether the debts to be taken over by the national government were to be the debts incurred during the war or those incurred after the war, down to 1790. Some states, mostly in the South — Georgia and North Carolina, for example — had very small debts. They opposed having the national government take them over while the New England states, which had huge debts, favored the idea. Bitter debates delayed any action for months.

Hamilton then appealed to Thomas Jefferson. The two sat down over the dinner table and worked out a deal. Jefferson agreed to back Hamilton's plan for the federal government to take over the state debts. Hamilton pledged to back the proposal to have the national capital located on the banks of the Potomac River, where it is today. With both leaders agreed, the debt proposal was adopted by Congress. To pay off the debt which the new national government had assumed, Congress in 1795 created a sinking fund — a fund set up to pay debts — which was to be built up from certain sums of money received by the government from taxes. Paying off the old debts and funding the new ones put the credit of the new government on a solid footing.

The Bank

☆☆ HAMILTON KNEW HE HAD WON ONLY THE FIRST ROUND. HE came back fighting. He next proposed that Congress charter a national bank. His idea was modeled after the Bank of England, which had done so much to make that country a world leader in finance. Hamilton's national bank was to be no ordinary bank. It was to be enabled to do far more than was usual. It was to issue notes to put money into circulation, to get loans for the government, to make tax collecting easier, and to make it easier to borrow money in general. The government was to put up one-fifth of the bank's capital of ten million dollars and was to have a say in running the bank.

The notion of a great central bank came as a shock to Virginians such as Madison and Jefferson. They wanted America to remain a nation of farmers. They did not want it to get into the hands of bankers and businessmen. Hamilton dreamed of America as a giant industrial country. Again Congress followed Hamilton, and passed the bank bill.

Now the question was up to President Washington. Should he sign the bill or veto it? Washington was not sure. He first turned to Jefferson for advice. Jefferson told him that the Constitution did not spell out any power to charter a bank and that such a bill was against the Constitution.

Hamilton, in turn, was consulted. He drew up one of his great state papers in which he demolished Jefferson's arguments. He maintained that the power given to Congress "to make all laws which shall be necessary and proper for carrying into execution the foregoing powers" — the so-called "necessary and proper clause" — covered such "needful" or "useful" matters as a bank. Hamilton won the day. Washington signed the bank bill. As it turned out, the bank was well run and of much value both to the government and to business. Even Hamilton's opponents recognized the strength of his argument. When Jefferson became President, he made no attempt to do away with the bank, and, in his turn, President Madison admitted that Congress had the authority to charter the bank.

The Whisky Rebellion

☆☆ SO FAR, HAMILTON HAD THINGS HIS WAY, BUT HE SOON ran into bigger trouble. Hamilton now proposed various taxes to support the government. Among them was a tax on distilled liquor. This tax hit the people in the western parts of the country much harder than it did those in the East. The eastern distillers of liquor had no trouble in passing on the tax to the consumers of the liquor by charging more for their product. The backwoods farmers living west of the Allegheny Mountains found it much too costly to ship their bulky grains to the East. It was much cheaper to distill the grain into liquor and ship it that way. Now they felt that this tax singled them out. Indeed, it was a heavy tax, amounting to nine dollars on each gallon of whisky.

26

The backwoods farmers were angered by the tax.

In 1794, the angry farmers of western Pennsylvania defied the law, captured a tax collector, and prevented the courts from sitting. "We have a full-scale insurrection on our hands," Hamilton told Washington. In letters to the press, Hamilton denounced the beginning of a reign of lawlessness that he called "anarchy." The war against the "whisky boys," as the western Pennsylvania protesters were called, was an unusual one. It was the only time in American history when a President actually took the field with his troops. Washington did so as commander in chief of the armed forces under the Constitution. It so happened that Secretary of War Knox was absent from his office. Hamilton had himself made Acting Secretary of War and took the field in person. Neither Washington, Hamilton, nor any of their men saw any fighting. Most of the whisky boys vanished on news that the army was marching. Those who stood their ground were merely carrying liberty poles, not guns. The leaders of the insurrection fled across the Ohio River. Only a few prisoners were taken. Two of them were tried and found guilty of high treason. Washington very wisely pardoned both of them, one on the ground that he was a "simpleton," the other on the ground that he was "insane."

Whether or not there was a real insurrection may still be a matter of debate, but Washington had shown the country the power of the federal government. The cost may well have been high because public opinion was divided over the strong-arm methods used to crush the tax protesters. In fact, the Whisky Rebellion can be singled out as a turning point in the fortunes of the Federalists.

Keeping Out of War

☆☆ WASHINGTON WANTED TO KEEP THE COUNTRY AT PEACE. His administration had to watch its step continually so as not to be drawn into the wars of other nations. As early as the summer of 1789, war between Spain and England seemed about to break out over disputed claims in the northwest Pacific. At that time, New Orleans, Florida, and Louisiana were all Spanish possessions. Since there was little way for England to attack these three Spanish areas without moving its North American troops across the United States, there seemed to be a grave danger that America would be drawn into the war against her will. Fortunately, Spain backed down, and the war threat ended.

The French Revolution brought on a reign of terror.

The French Revolution and America

☆☆ A GREAT DANGER WAS POSED TO THE LIFE OF THE NEW NA-
tion by the French Revolution, which broke out in 1789, and
by the wars between France and England that followed in its
wake. At first, the news of the revolution in France was hailed
in America. It seemed like the kind of uprising for which America herself had only recently set the example. But the situation
became alarming when the various rulers of Europe joined
forces to put down the French Revolution. In turn, a move-
ment against the royalists took place in France and led to the
execution of King Louis XVI and his wife, Marie Antoinette.
This execution was followed by a reign of terror in which many
persons of all French parties were put to death.

On February 1, 1793, France declared war on England. America was bound to France by a treaty of alliance made in 1778. Was America obliged to enter the war as an ally of France? Thomas Jefferson held that the treaty was still binding. Alexander Hamilton insisted that the treaty had been made with Louis XVI and that once the former French government had been overthrown, the alliance was no longer in force.

Washington Proclaims Neutrality

☆☆ ONCE MORE, OVER THE OBJECTIONS OF JEFFERSON, WASHington followed the advice of Hamilton. In 1793, he issued his momentous Proclamation of Neutrality. In this document he declared that the United States intended to be friendly and impartial to both warring powers and asked that all citizens follow that course.

Could the United States remain neutral in the face of great pressures? The question did not have to wait long to be put to the test. The new French minister to the United States was "Citizen" Edmond Genêt. After he arrived in America and before he called upon the President, he spent a good deal of time in speaking on behalf of France. He attempted to organize bases in the United States from which the French navy might operate, and he tried to recruit sailors for French ships. Even Madison, who was a member of the pro-French party, declared that Genêt had acted like a madman. When Genêt saw that Thomas Jefferson had lost patience with him, he threatened to appeal to the American people over the heads of their leaders. Washington's Cabinet united in demanding that Genêt be recalled to France. Since the members of the Cabinet realized that France was in a reign of terror and that Genêt would be headed for the guillotine — a very fancy French chopping block — Washington allowed him to live in New York as a private person.

Jefferson was hurt that Genêt had let him down. He was even more hurt that Washington had ignored his advice. He now decided to resign as Secretary of State. He was succeeded in January 1794, by Edmund Randolph.

Jay's Treaty

☆☆ IT WAS HARD ENOUGH TO AVOID TROUBLE WITH FRANCE. The troubles with England, however, were of much longer standing. Neither England nor the United States had carried out in full the terms of the Treaty of Paris of 1783, which ended the American Revolution. Britain still kept her troops on the American frontier. She still refused to pay for the black slaves she had removed from America during the Revolution.

The United States, for its part, had failed to get the states to protect British creditors. It had not been able to stop the states from taking over the properties of the Loyalists. Finally, no commercial agreement between the United States and England could be worked out. There were strained relations

Men from British warships seized American seamen.

between the two countries over all these matters.

Washington had to send troops to the Northwest Territory to put down Indian uprisings. This was no easy task, but in 1794, Revolutionary War hero General Anthony Wayne defeated the Indians at Fallen Timbers in northwest Ohio. As a result, the Indians made a treaty with the United States in which they gave up all the claims that they had to the Ohio region.

On the high seas, the war between England and France took its toll of American ships and American seamen. Some three hundred American ships were seized by the royal navy for carrying grain and flour to France. In addition, the British stopped American ships on the high seas and took off sailors, to make them serve on British warships. If the sailors could not prove that they were American citizens, the British navy took it for granted that they were Englishmen because they spoke English. This seizing of seamen was the hated practice of impressment.

What could be done? Jefferson proposed that the United States should refuse to admit into its country any goods from England. Such a step is known as a boycott. Hamilton knew that a boycott would cause the United States to lose the revenue that it had been gaining from the tariff on imported goods. He regarded the tariff as the main prop for his elaborate financial system and felt that upsetting commercial relations between the two countries would cut America's credit to the roots. George Washington did not want a trade war, either. He felt that the United States and England should try to settle their grievances peacefully. For that difficult task, he turned to Chief Justice John Jay. In 1794, Jay was ordered to go to England and to work for a treaty by which England would agree to get out of the military posts in the Northwest Territory, would allow American ships to travel peacefully on the high seas, and would pay damages for ships that had been seized.

The United States was not the only country that did not like England's high-handed rule on the seas. In Europe, a League of Neutral Nations was founded to secure the freedom of the seas. Had America joined the League, this country could have been something of a threat to England. Without Jay's knowing it, Hamilton told George Hammond, the young British minister to the United States, that England had nothing to worry about and that America would not join the League. Hamilton was so concerned about keeping trade moving between England and America that he helped cut the ground from under Jay's feet. As a result, Jay was only able to get the British to agree to do things that they had more or less planned to do already. For example, the British agreed to withdraw from the posts in the Northwest Territory. They agreed to open up the East Indies to American shipping. But so far as the British West Indies were concerned, American shippers were to be restricted to small boats that were forbidden to carry the chief products that were raised on those islands.

The most novel feature of Jay's Treaty — and the one that had the most lasting results — was Jay's provision for setting up commissions to decide on the disputed northeastern boundary and certain creditors' claims that had arisen before the American Revolution. The idea of having a commission of persons from both sides or even from a third nation to settle disputed matters was to be used many times by the United States in the years to come.

When Washington saw the treaty, he was quite disappointed. It did not end the impressment of seamen; it did not give damages to Americans for slaves that had been removed or to Loyalists for properties that had been seized. While the President may not have been very happy, the American public was shocked on learning the terms of Jay's Treaty. A mob stoned Hamilton, and others burned John Jay in effigy. Somebody chalked on the fence of a Massachusetts lawyer: "Damn John Jay! Damn anyone who won't damn John Jay! Damn anyone who won't put lights in his window and sit up all night damning John Jay!"

The enemies of the treaty seemed to have everything their way, but they had not counted on Alexander Hamilton. At Washington's request, Hamilton wrote a series of famous letters to the people in which he defended the treaty. Appearing in the New York *Argus* in 1795, they were signed "Camillus," but in them readers recognized Hamilton's masterly style.

After very long and bitter debate, the Senate ratified the treaty but dropped the article relating to the West Indian trade. Jefferson and the other opponents of the treaty did not give up easily. They now turned to the House of Representatives and sought to prevent any money from being voted to carry out the provisions of the treaty. At this point, Fisher Ames, an eloquent Federalist congressman from New England,

A mob burned John Jay in effigy.

delivered one of the greatest orations in the history of Congress. He warned that the Union would collapse and war break out should the treaty fail. The House heeded Ames and, by a narrow margin, voted the money.

As we look back on it, we can realize that Jay's Treaty was a good thing for the young nation. It gave the United States full control in law, and, in fact over the Northwest Territory. It prevented a war that could have brought disaster to the country. It started what amounted to ten years of friendly relations with Great Britain. It had one other effect, too. When the members of the Spanish royal court heard of Jay's Treaty, they were terror-stricken. Did Jay's Treaty really mean that England and America were secretly in alliance? If that were the case, then America's frontiersmen could turn against the Southwest and take it from Spain. Worried by the longer-range meanings of the treaty, the Spanish court courteously received Thomas Pinckney, a special envoy from the United States. The Spaniards now agreed to allow Americans to navigate the Mississippi River freely and to place goods on deposit in Spanish New Orleans — two things the Americans had hitherto been unable to do. Spain also recognized the Mississippi River as the western boundary of the United States and the 31st parallel as the southern boundary. As a result, a long struggle by the Americans to use the Mississippi River and to obtain living room west of the mountains came to a triumphant climax.

Parties Are Born

☆☆ NOBODY EXPECTED THAT OPPOSING POLITICAL PARTIES would be formed so soon. As a matter of fact, the Founding Fathers thought parties were not good for the nation as they divided people instead of uniting them. But within a very few years, parties appeared, with Alexander Hamilton as the leader of the Federalists and James Madison as the manager of the opposing party, which supported Jefferson's program and was known as the Democratic-Republican or just plain Republican party. Jefferson drew his support chiefly from the farmers. Virginia tobacco planters felt that it was unfair that they should be made to pay back to their British enemies the debts contracted before the Revolution. They thought it a shame that anyone should profit by inside knowledge of what the government was going to do. They believed in a federal government with limited power — a central government that would be careful not to encroach upon the rights of the states.

Hamilton's Federalists counted on the loyal backing of northern businessmen. They favored Hamilton's policies, believed that debtors should be made to pay their debts, and that the government of the country should be left in the hands of the "wise and good."

While it is not easy to say when parties began, it is clear that they had appeared by 1792. By that time, Cabinet meetings were marred by quarrels. Jefferson said that he and Hamilton were "pitted against each other every day in the Cabinet like two fighting cocks." Hamilton, in turn, accused Jefferson of being pro-French and ambitious of becoming President.

Both sides were continually engaged in attacking each other. Both sides had their own paid editors and their own newspapers, and there was much regrettable mudslinging. The Republicans were tireless in seeking to show that Hamilton was corrupt, but they were unsuccessful. They even spoke harshly of Washington for supporting Hamilton's policies. The Republicans, who were anxious to turn the Federalists out of office, worked night and day to build a strong party machine in town and country. Madison and Jefferson proved to be the first great party organizers in American history.

Washington Says Farewell to the Nation

☆☆ AT THE END OF HIS SECOND TERM AS PRESIDENT, WASH-
ington made the big decision not to stand for a third term.
Until Franklin D. Roosevelt was elected to a third term in
1940, Washington's "no-third-term" stand was accepted as an
unwritten law of the Constitution. In fact, it has now been put
into the Constitution as the twenty-second amendment, adopted in 1951. Since then, no President can serve more than two
terms.

Washington put a great deal of time into writing a farewell
message to the nation. He had first consulted James Madison,
who prepared a draft of the message for him. Washington made
some lengthy notes of his own on this draft and sent the cor-

rections and additions to Alexander Hamilton, who consulted John Jay, as Washington had asked him to. Hamilton prepared two drafts, carefully following Washington's main ideas but rewording them in a masterly way. Washington picked what he wanted from these drafts and made important changes. He never read his Farewell Address to the public but sent it to a Philadelphia newspaper, the *Daily American Advertiser*. There it appeared on September 19, 1796.

The Farewell Address is one of America's great state papers. Some of Washington's advice was not heeded. He warned against factions but could not prevent the two-party system from arising. He warned against the danger that different sections of the country might take opposing positions on public questions. This was a prophetic warning of the terrible civil war that was later to break out between the North and the South.

Washington's most lasting advice was contained in his "Great Rule." For a long time, this proved to be the basis of America's foreign policy. In his Proclamation of Neutrality and in Jay's Treaty with Great Britain, President Washington had shown the country that avoiding war was the best policy for the nation. In the Farewell Address, he laid it down as "our true policy to steer clear of permanent alliances with any portion of the foreign world, so far, I mean, as we are now at liberty to do it." He did not bar "occasional alliances for extraordinary war emergencies." In other words, he was a man who saw things as they were and did not take a position that was unchangeable. He was talking about conditions in the world of his day and did not mean to impose a rule for all time.

Still, the "Great Rule" concerning foreign policy was the most cherished principle of American diplomacy. Nobody dared tamper with it until the twentieth century, when terrible new perils made it necessary for America to assume a large role in world affairs.

John Adams as the Second President

☆☆ THE FIRST REAL CONTEST FOR THE PRESIDENCY WAS touched off by the announcement that Washington would retire at the end of his second term. The Republicans picked Thomas Jefferson as their candidate for President and Aaron Burr, a New York lawyer, for Vice President. The Federalists picked John Adams for the top post and Thomas Pinckney of South Carolina for the second spot. When the ballots were counted, Adams had seventy-one votes; Jefferson, sixty-eight; Pinckney, fifty-nine; and Burr, thirty.

Adams, the stocky lawyer from Braintree, Massachusetts, was sixty-two years old when he took office. Years before, he had given up his legal practice and had devoted himself entire-

John
Adams

ly to the affairs of his country. He had been one of the first and foremost patriots. He had written the famous Massachusetts Constitution of 1780. Along with a badly needed loan, he had secured from the Dutch nation a recognition of the thirteen states as an independent nation. He had been one of the American commissioners who had made the peace with England ending the Revolutionary War. He had then served as America's minister to England, doing what he could to smooth relations between the mother country and her former colonies.

To work with John Adams was no easy task. He could be testy, prickly, vain, and even jealous of men with talent equal to his own. But he had a wonderful sense of humor, an enormous amount of ability, and a first-class mind. He was so frank that people called him "Honest John" Adams.

The slender margin by which Adams had been elected President should have served as a warning to him that the people were no longer united behind the foreign policy of the Federalists. Adams started out by making his biggest error. He did not pick his own Cabinet but allowed the members of Washington's Cabinet to stay on. These men owed their loyalty to Alexander Hamilton and not to the new President, and they proved a constant source of trouble to Adams.

Adams as a Man of Peace

☆☆ THE BIG PROBLEM FACING ADAMS WAS HOW TO IMPROVE America's relations with France. When the terms of Jay's Treaty became known, the French were furious. The French minister to the United States, Pierre Adet, worked to defeat the ratification of the treaty. Quite openly he campaigned for Jefferson's election in 1796.

Even though Adams knew that the French had no love for him, he decided to try to patch up the quarrel. In 1797, he picked three men to be sent on a delicate mission to Paris. John Marshall of Virginia (later Chief Justice) and Elbridge Gerry of Massachusetts joined Charles C. Pinckney of South Carolina in Paris. There they met with three secret agents of the French government. These agents were so secret that in reports to the United States government they were designated by ciphers — "X" (Hottinguer), "Y" (Bellamy), and "Z" (Hauteval).

If the Americans expected to be received by the French government, the agents told them, they would first have to pay a bribe to French officials, make a loan to France, and admit that President Adams was wrong in criticizing the French government. According to legend, the American commissioners rose in their wrath and declared: "Millions for defense, but not one cent for tribute!" This may be a heroic version of what was really said. Pinckney is supposed to have answered the French agents: "It is no, no; not a sixpence!"

The inside story of the XYZ affair burst like a bombshell on the American political scene. Hamilton warned that anybody who would now support France was not an American but "a fool, a madman, or a traitor." Every French flag was pulled down from the coffeehouses, and the pro-French Republicans were in full retreat.

Now was the time to declare war against France, Timothy Pickering, the Secretary of State, advised President Adams. Up to a point, Adams went along. He named George Washington commanding general of the army and Hamilton inspector general and second in command. In July 1798, Congress repealed the treaties with France. The famous alliance of the American Revolution was now at an end. On the seas, a naval war between France and the United States began without being formally declared, and a number of French ships were captured.

French flags were pulled down from the coffeehouses.

52

Through it all, Adams kept cool, as a President should. When he realized at long last that Hamilton was giving orders to the Cabinet behind his back, he decided to act on his own. He was told indirectly that France would welcome an American envoy. Adams went ahead and named William Vans Murray for the task, then added Chief Justice Oliver Ellsworth and Governor William R. Davie of North Carolina.

Adams had made the big and correct decision, but it cost him what little popularity he may have had. The man in the street cried out for war, and Hamilton screamed more frantically than ever. Adams now fired his Secretary of State and Secretary of War, replacing them with men loyal to himself. With the chief haters of France out of the Cabinet, Adams had paved the way for the agreement soon reached with that country to end the quarrel between the two nations. Adams regarded his stand on war with France as "the most successful of my whole life." History supports him.

Civil Liberties in Time of Crisis

☆☆ THE RECORD OF THE ADAMS' PRESIDENCY IS NOT AS HAPPY a one on the domestic side as on the foreign. The Federalists were so alarmed about the dangers posed to America by France and the French that they acted hysterically. They rammed through Congress four laws that are known as the Alien and Sedition Acts. These acts greatly lengthened the time required before a foreigner could become an American citizen. They gave the President the power to expel from the country any foreigner (alien) whom he thought dangerous, and to arrest or banish any enemy alien in time of war. Finally, the Sedition Act, among other things, made it a crime to publish false statements about the government.

Under this act, the courts soon began to punish leading critics of the government, such as Republican newspaper editors. These unfortunates were fined and imprisoned, often after shockingly unfair trials.

The Republicans made the best of the Federalists' mistakes. The legislatures of Kentucky and Virginia adopted resolutions that Thomas Jefferson and James Madison had drawn up. These resolutions denounced the Alien and Sedition Acts as being against the Constitution. They pointed out that where the national government exceeded its powers, each state had a right to judge for itself what steps to take to get redress. In a second resolution, the Kentucky legislature asserted that the states had a right to nullify the acts of the national government.

The Republicans had, in fact, gone too far, and the nation was to rue the day that these extreme views of states' rights were expressed.

The End of the Federalists

★★ THE CRISIS OVER FRANCE PROVED THE UNDOING OF THE Federalists. The man in the street was shocked at the trials and punishments meted out to the foes of the government. The government itself was sharply divided over the handling of the crisis. If Adams saved the country from war, he lost his own party by so doing. Hamilton and the high Federalists around him now worked in every possible way to prevent Adams from being reelected President in 1800. Hamilton went so far as to publish under his own name an unfair and unwise attack on Adams. With his party badly split, Adams lost his bid for reelection in 1800. Thomas Jefferson was the nation's choice to succeed him as the third President.

The victory of Jefferson in 1800 showed that the Federalists had lost the confidence of the people; the Federalist party was never again to capture the Presidency. One might well ask why a group that had done so much to start the Union on a strong footing should suddenly decline and never recover the lost ground. In answer, it might be said that somehow its leaders and its methods now seemed old-fashioned. The Federalists had lost trust in the people, and the people had lost confidence in them. A new era was emerging when leaders closer to the people would shape the nation's destinies. The Federalists had won a permanent place in the hearts of the people, but their time had passed, and they themselves knew it.

No one can overlook their magnificent accomplishments, however. They showed that the Constitution could be made to work. They settled the powers of the Presidency. They invented the American cabinet system. They set up the federal courts. They taxed the people for the national good. They put the country's credit on a firm base. They cleared American territory of the British and Spanish forces that had stayed on the frontier after the Revolutionary War. Most important, they kept the new nation from making a terrible mistake. They saw to it that the United States did not get drawn into the wars that swept Europe from end to end with the start of the French Revolution.

There Were Giants in Those Days

☆☆ AT THE END OF HIS TERM, GEORGE WASHINGTON, WORN out by his arduous Presidential duties, had returned to Mount Vernon. On December 12, 1799, he mounted his horse and made the usual rounds of his estate. Snow, which had begun to fall, covered his head and greatcoat. The next morning, he complained of a sore throat. That night he was shaken with chills, and his throat was becoming more painful. He was given a combination of vinegar, molasses, and butter, but he could not swallow. Doctors were called in, and, after the fashion of the time, they bled their patient copiously. No worse treatment could have been applied. The General's condition slowly worsened. He knew he was dying. "I die hard, but I am not afraid to go," he is supposed to have remarked. Death came about two hours before midnight of December 14, 1799. The General was buried in the simple family vault on the slope of Mount Vernon. His death plunged the nation into deep mourning. Save for Benjamin Franklin, who had died back in 1790 at the age of eighty-four, Washington was the first of the Revolutionary immortals to leave the scene of his great activities. The nation hailed him as *Pater Patriae* — Father of his Country.

Alexander Hamilton was the next of the Federalists to go. In 1804, he was challenged to a duel by Aaron Burr, an old political foe of Hamilton's and the Vice President in Jefferson's first administration. Hamilton had called Burr a man "who ought not to be trusted with the reins of government." (History has proved Hamilton right.) He refused to apologize to Burr. The duel was fought in Weehawken, New Jersey. Hamilton planned not to fire at Burr but to fire into the air instead. Burr had different ideas. He aimed to put an end to his hated rival's career and did so with his first shot. Hamilton must have expected the worst. On the night before the fatal duel, he wrote Elizabeth Schuyler Hamilton a sweet note, ending, "Adieu, my darling wife."

Hamilton was widely mourned as one of the brightest stars in American government, even though some of his ideas had come to seem out of place in the democratic republic of Thomas Jefferson.

After his Presidency, "Honest John" Adams never held public office again. For years he lived in retirement at Brain-

Aaron
Burr

tree, Massachusetts. He carried on a wonderful letter-writing exchange with an old political foe but still good friend, Thomas Jefferson. He lived to see his eldest son, John Quincy Adams, become the sixth President of the United States. He died on July 4, 1826, fifty years to the day from the time that the Declaration of Independence was adopted. His last words were, "Thomas Jefferson survives." He did not know that Thomas Jefferson had passed away only a few hours before him at his home at Monticello, Virginia.

The patriotic John Jay had resigned as Chief Justice to serve for two terms as governor of New York State. Thereafter he lived in quiet retirement at his country home at Bedford, New York. He devoted himself to the cause of the black slaves and to religion. He died in 1829 at the age of eighty-four.

Last of the Founding Fathers, James Madison lived on until 1836. In his parting counsel to his country, the aged patriot wrote: "The advice nearest to my heart and deepest in my convictions is that the Union of the United States be cherished and perpetuated."

The Age of Giants had passed. But the heroic efforts of the Founding Fathers had done much to make the experiment of the American republic a success. They shall not be forgotten.

INDEX

RICHARD B. MORRIS, Gouverneur Morris Professor of History Emeritus at Columbia University, is one of the United States' foremost authorities in the field of American history. He has also taught or lectured at many other universities, including Princeton, the University of Hawaii, and the John F. Kennedy Institute in West Berlin, and is a three-time recipient of a Guggenheim Fellowship. In addition, Dr. Morris is editor of the *Encyclopedia of American History* and the author of numerous books, including the Bancroft Award winner, *The Peacemakers*, and *Witnesses at the Creation: Hamilton, Madison, Jay, and the Constitution*. Presently, he is co-chair of *Project '87*, a nationwide organization devoted to commemorating the 200th anniversary of the U.S. Constitution.

AMERICAN HISTORY TOPIC BOOKS

The American Revolution
The Constitution
The Founding of the Republic
The Indian Wars
The War of 1812